My First
TONGAN
200 Picture Word Book
with English translations

GERÅRD AFLÅGUE COLLECTION

Designed by
Gerard Aflague

Tongan translations by East-West Concepts
www.eastwestconcepts.com

Published by the
GERÅRD AFLÅGUE COLLECTION
Copyright 2016, 2018

All rights reserved. No part of this book may be reproduced, stored in a retrieval system, or transmitted in any form by any means, without written permission from the publisher.

Foreword

We realize that folks across the world seek resources to learn and teach the language of the natives of Tonga. Our passion is not only to create language learning books, but to also share them across the world with those that have a desire to discover what it is all about. We hope that this title offers you something special to invigorate curious and maleable minds of children who desire to learn and grow. Share this book with your friends and family, and spread your love for the Tongan culture through language.

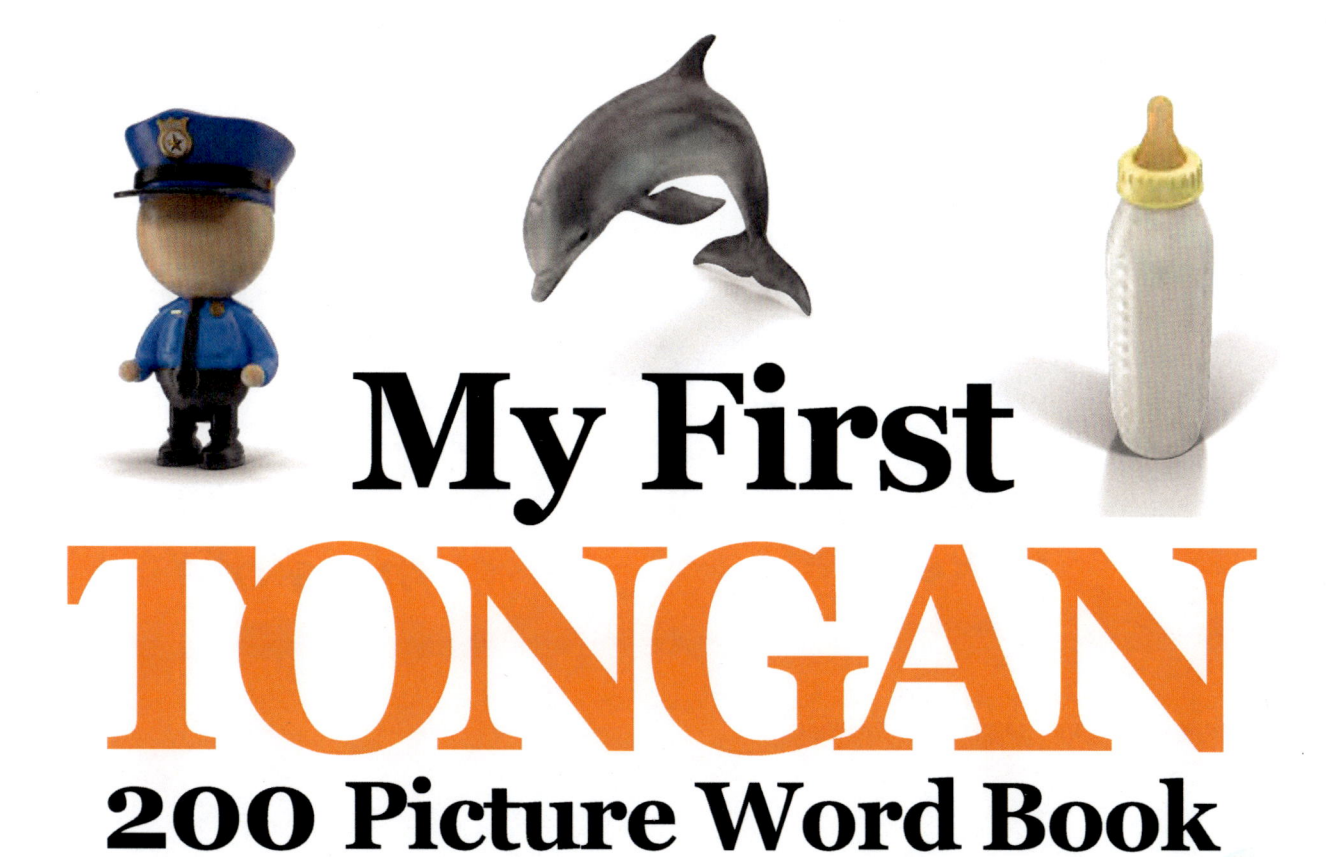

My First
TONGAN
200 Picture Word Book
with English translations

GERÅRD AFLÅGUE COLLECTION

cake
keke

gift
me'a'ofa

coconut tree
fu'u niu

canoe
pōpao

basketball
fo'i pulu pasiketipolo

apple
'apele

key
kī

fish
ika

car
kā

toothbrush
pōlosi fufulu nifo

house
fale

rat
kūma

cloud
'ao

whale
tofua'a

starfish
sitafisi

bulldozer
pulutousa

slippers
silipa

bicycle
pasikala

book
tohi

baby bottle
hina huhu pepee

policeman
pōlisi tangata

submarine
vakauku

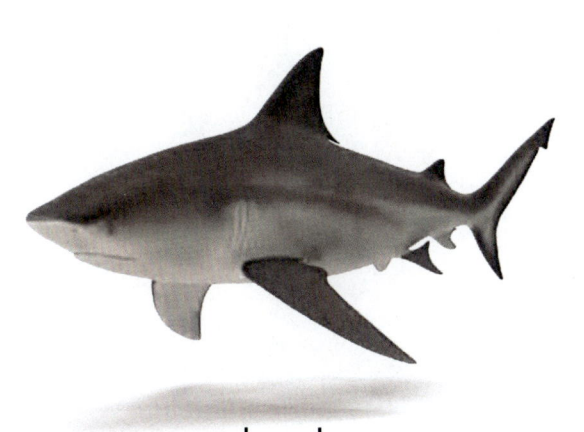

shark
'anga

tree
fu'u 'akau

flag
fuka

cat
pusi

banana
siaine

Santa claus
sanitā kolosi

money
pa'anga

plane
vakapuna

firetruck
loli tāmate afi

toilet bowl
pō falemālolo

ant
lō

hat
tātaa

newspaper
nusipepa

bus
pasi

table
tepile

heart
fo'imafu

box
nge'esi puha

lunch bag
kato lanisi

purse
kato peesi

tire
fo'i va'e me'alele

coin
koini

shoe
sū

notepad
noutipuka

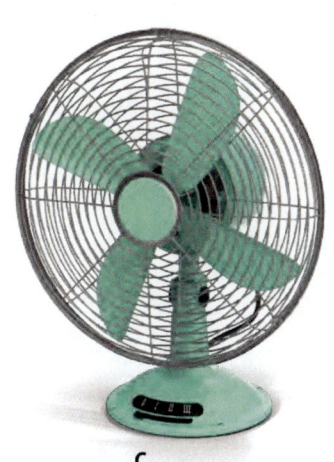

fly
lango

fan
ii 'uhila

bag
pepa peeki

ice cream
'aisikilimi

waste basket
kato veve

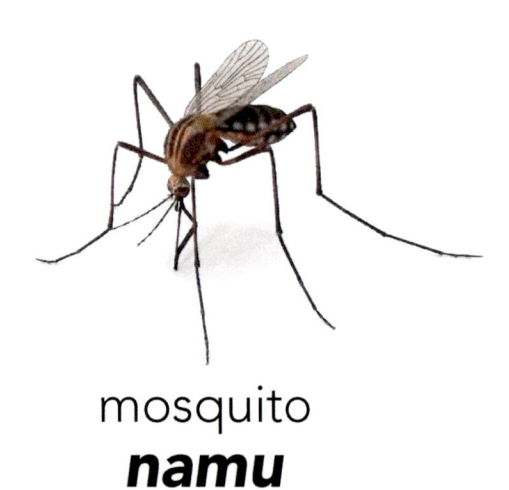

mosquito
namu

rock
fo'imaka

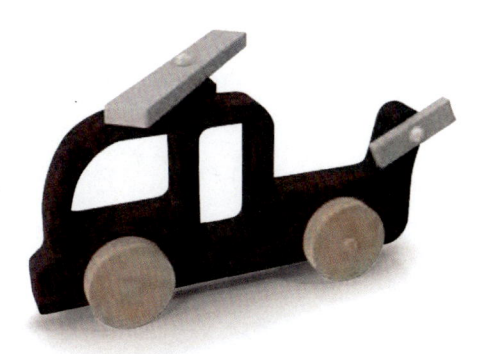

helicopter
helekopeta

doctor
toketa

couch
sea sofa

glass
ipu sio'ata

jet ski
seti sikii

fork
huhu

star
fo'i fetu'u

wagon
ki'i saliote taulani

baby shoes
sū pepee

fruit
fu'ai'akau fuluti

pineapple
fainā

bread basket
kato ma

bell
fafangu

firewood
fefie

paper plane
vakapuna pepa

sun
la'a

map
mape

snail
sineili

flowers
matala'i'akau

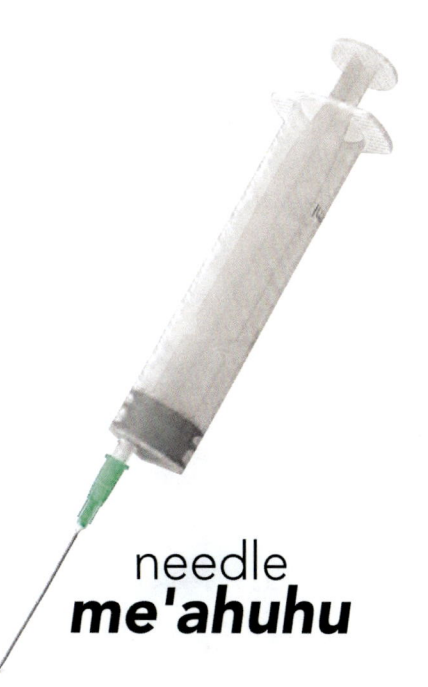

needle
me'ahuhu

clock
'uasi

boat
vaka

candle
te'elango

bed
mōhenga

spoon
sēpuni

turtle
fonu

stick
va'a 'akau

stairs
sitepu

laptop
leepi topu

grass
mūsie

plate
peleti

teddy bear
teti pea

paint
kapa vali

pen
polopeni

horse
hoosi

pool
vai kaukau

umbrella
fakamalu

hammer
hāmala

ladder
tu'unga

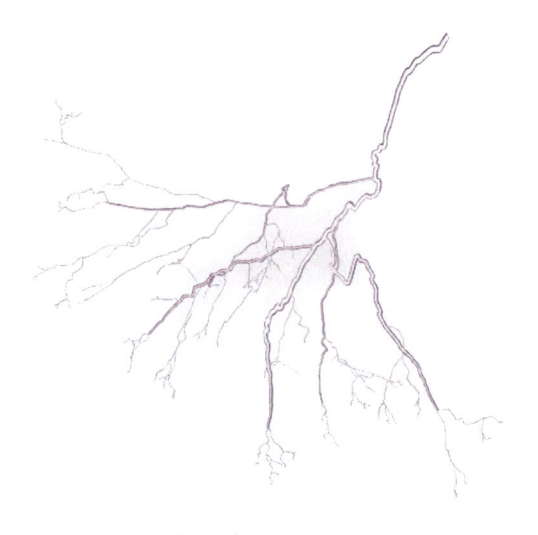

lightning
maama fatulisi uhila

crayons
kala tavalivali

cookie
kukisi

hot air balloon
pula fakamalu 'ea

scissors
helekosi

egg
fua'imoa

bird
manupuna

kite
lofa

baby stroller
saliote pepee

snake
ngata

rope
maea

moon
māhina

chair
sea

elephant
'elefanite

clam
fingota mehingo

cross
kolosi

fire hydrant
paipa tamate afi

cement block
fo'i piliki

soap
koa

frog
poto

light switch
me'a kamosi 'uhila

popsicle
'aisi poloka

milk carton
puha hu'akau

chocolate candy
pa lole sokoleti

corn
koane

coffee beans
kofi piini

drawer
toloa vala

baby food
me'akai pepee

computer
komipiuta

diver
tangata uku

ring
mama

hair brush
polosi 'ulu

judge
Tu'i Fakamaau

soldier
sōtia

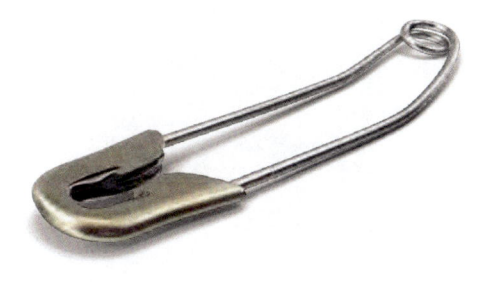

shirt
sote

pin
fo'i pine napikeni

sunglasses
matasio'ata

candy
lole keniti

meat
kakano'i manu

Earth
mamani

television
televisone

dining table
tepile kai

saw
kili tutu'u

mirror
sio'ata

plant
'fu'u 'akau

shovel
sāvolo

washer
misini fō

lawn mower
misini kosi

crib
mōhenga pepee

flash light
me'a hulu kasa

picture frame
'esia'i tā

towel
tauveli

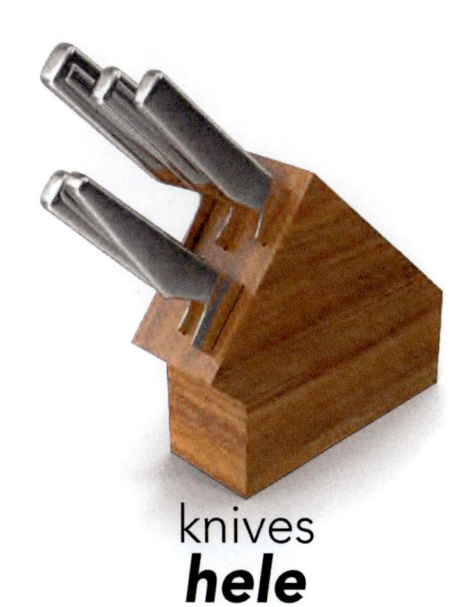

knives
hele

refrigerator
'aisi tu'u

gas pump
pamu pausa

paper towel
pepa taueli

lamp shade
maama tu'u

pillow
pilo

sugar
suka

barbecue grill
me'atunu papakiu

chopping board
pooti papa hifi

light bulb
fo'i'uhila

trash truck
loli veve

baseball mit
kofu nima peisipolo

dog bowl
poulu kulii

book shelf
papa hili'anga tohi

food container
peleti me'akai

carpet
kapeti

sea horse
hoosi tahi

can
kapa

neck tie
hekesi

hospital
falemahaki

comb
helu 'ulu

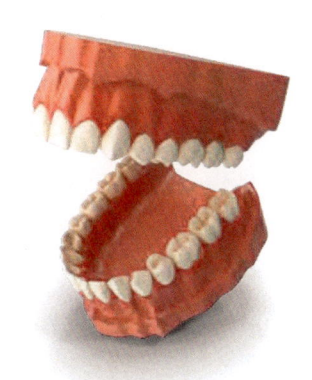

false teeth
nifo loi

camera
me'a faita

bee
pī

guitar
kitaa

jellyfish
kolukalu

stingray
ika koe fai

lobster
'fo'i 'uo

candle
te'elango

octopus
feke

office
'loki 'ofisi

bank
pangike

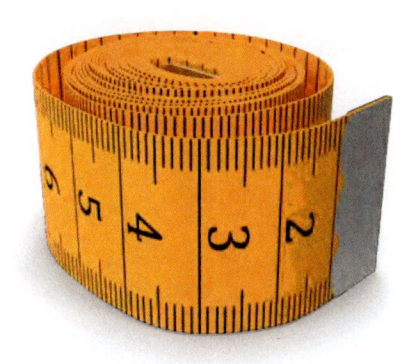

measuring tape
tepi fua

green beans
piini lanumata

onion
onioni

deer
tia

dragonfly
lango puna

hammerhead shark
'anga 'ulu hamala

diamond
taiamoni

roses
mata'ilose

cockroach
mongomonga

potato
pateta

rocking chair
sea selue

cleaver
hele tofi

anchor
taula

eggplant
paingani

diapers
taipa

grapes
kalepi

paper clip
pepa kilipa

dolphin
tolofini

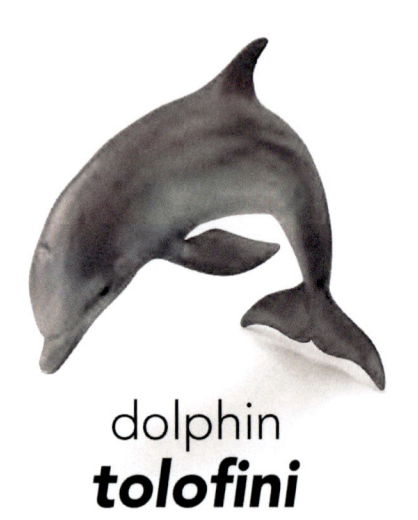

scorpion
sikapio

music
nota hiva

door
matapa

spider
hina

carrot
kaloti

swing
selue heke

coral
feo

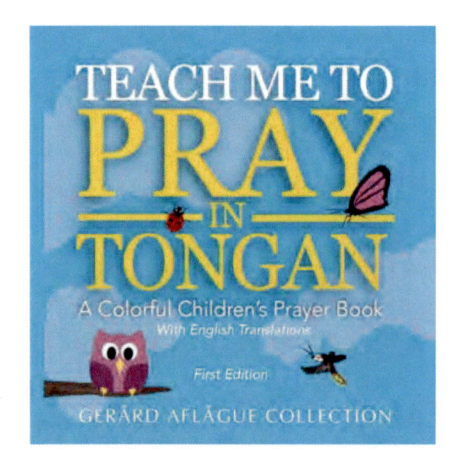

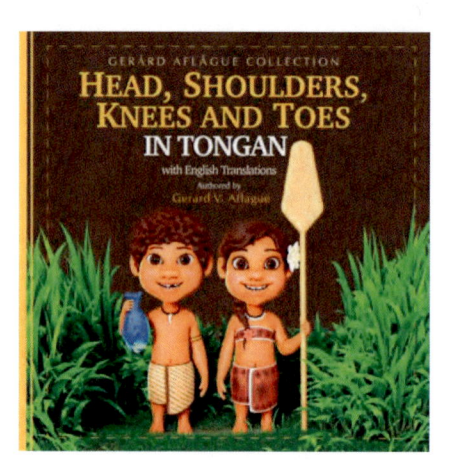

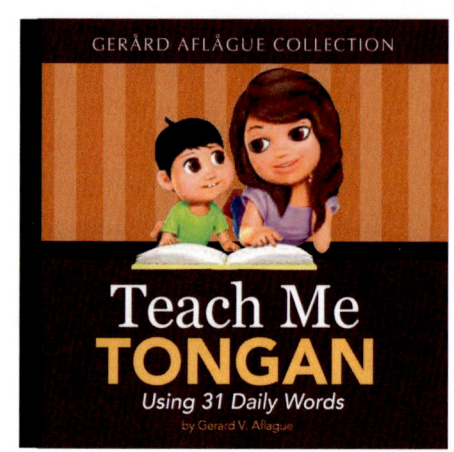

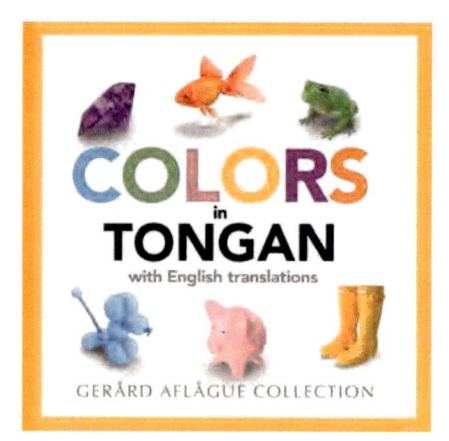

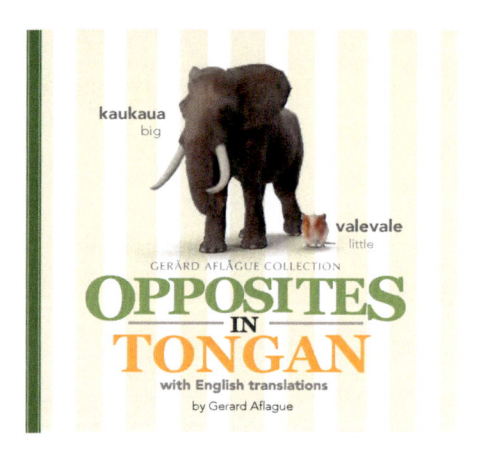

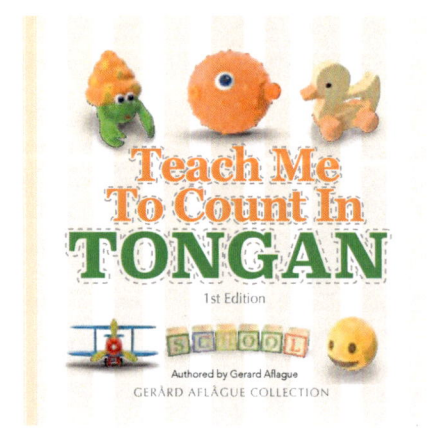

We enjoy hearing directly from our customers. Feel free to email us at sales@gerardaflaguecollection.com.

New Tongan titles are being released on a regular basis. Shop online.

About the Author

Mary Aflague was born and raised on the beautiful island of Guam. Now residing in Colorado, she still manages to enjoy the outdoors and sunshine. She is a long time educator and continues to instill in her children and students, the joy and power of being life-long readers and learners. Her interests include reading, yoga, art, traveling, and Pacific island dance.

About the Designer

Gerard Aflague is a long-time Guam native who resides in Highlands Ranch, Colorado. Gerard enjoys illustrating and publishing cultural books that inspire, educate, and entertain. He also helps others publish their books under his collection. In addition to publishing, he also writes, and is a product designer and inventor. In addition to his passions, he has a long and successful career in public service, in addition to managing his online retail company. When he is not dreaming up new products for his collection, he spends time with family traveling, enjoying good food, or reading a good book.

Made in the USA
San Bernardino, CA
28 April 2019